~KINGDOMMINDED~CREATIVE THINKING~

Bringing Your Vision into Manifestation

A BUSINESS GUIDE BASED ON

KINGDOM PRINCIPLES

CHANDA D. COSTON

KINGDOM CONCEPTS PUBLISHING CO.

KINGDOM MINDED

CREATIVE THINKING

Chanda D. Coston

.

Kingdom Concepts Publishing Co

www.KingdomConceptsIntl.org

Printed in the United States

I dedicate this work to my heavenly father who is

ALWAYS faithful and

my children who even in their innocence and youth

help me to walk out my dreams so that I may

help you to walk out yours....

"Hold fast to dreams, for if dreams die, life is a broken winged bird that cannot fly."

– Langston Hughes

Table of Contents

Introduction

~KINGDOMMINDED~CREATIVE THINKING~

Bringing Your Vision into Manifestation

Manifesting. . . . your Dreams. . ..

So many times, I have had conversations with people who say that they have a dream but they don't know how to make it happen. They want to make a living doing what they love by opening a business but don't know where to begin. I often tell people that if they tap into their purpose then it's there in their purpose that they will find their passion for life but also they will find their prosperity. When we pray and ask God to bless us in the area of prosperity, he often gives us an idea for wealth. Unfortunately, once we have the idea, we often don't know what we should do next. This manual is a guide to provide direction and instruction for those who are ready and willing to do go forward in their destiny. We will identify your goal and then provide the guidelines to writing out the steps on how to get there. If you want to start this journey of manifesting your dreams then join us. How far you go is up to you.

OVERVIEW

Of your goal

Overview, KNOW where you're going…

Overview *is a look at your process to SUCCESS.*

There is a saying that one of the richest

places in the world is the grave yards. It is

because so many people leave the earth

unfulfilled & carry their dreams & visions to their

graves. This manual is written to help you have a different outcome. It is to help you walk into your destiny. I don't claim any magical overnight success but I do have a proven formula that works if you simply follow the process. You can use it time and time again.

I work as a consultant & apart of what I do is called process improvement. I am brought into an organization to observe the current process & help companies find more efficient/productive ways to do what they are doing. In this same way, there are tons of people that have dreams but they do not know how to achieve them. Each year many people set out to achieve goals, start businesses, go back to school, save money etc. but fall short and can't figure out why. If you can relate to what I'm saying then this is for you.

I will help you to identify the road blocks in your process that are often overlooked by simply writing it down and mapping out the process (don't worry; I'll explain more on this later). The bible tells us that there is nothing new under the sun. This definitely isn't an exception to the rule. It says to write the vision & make it plain. It worked back then and it still works. This principle alone is huge in the success of your vision. It helps to keep you focused and on track. It also helps you identify the best route to take while maintaining a realistic timeline to complete your goal. In this manual, we will look at how you can do all of this to help you with your own success.

Now we will take a further look at how this applies to us as Christians & to do that I'm going to take you through a short exercise to help get our minds thinking in the right direction. *(Note: Studies have shown that when these exercises are done on a regular basis, those who do them often experience what it is they visualize in their minds).*

Visualization Exercise:

Close your eyes and get a part of your life in your mind that you desire to see something new. It can be anything at all. If it's a car for example. See it. Walk around it. Imagine the color. The body of it. The tires. Open the door & imagine yourself sitting inside of it. Imagine what the dashboard looks like. Imagine the color of the interior. The color and material of the seats. If it's a Ferrari than see yourself running your hand over the emblem, smell it. Lay back in it & feel it.

When you are done, open your eyes.

Question: What did you envision?

Answer: _____

Question: What's your dream/goal?

Answer: _____

Action: Spend 10-15 minutes per day envisioning yourself doing whatever it is that you desire to accomplish. You will find that you will have more creative thoughts in regards to how to accomplish this task. You will find that more doors and opportunities will seem to come your way because you will be more open to them and receiving them.

This is so powerful and we will take a look at why: We humans are made up of a physical body, a soul (emotion, will & intellect) & our spirit. Although all of these are important, we are going to look at two of our spiritual/eternal abilities that we have as spirit beings.

Spiritual Abilities:

- Thoughts

- Spoken words

Our thoughts have the power to take us into unknown places through our imagination. We have the ability to be creative and/or innovative simply by imagining in depth details. Our minds are so strong that what we see and/or imagine in our minds can make our bodies believe that it's real. This is often experienced in our dreams when we sleep. I believe that God did not intend for us to isolate this to just our dreams but for us to use it in our daily lives. Just as we are created in the very image and likeness of God; Just as He is The Creator, He has given us the ability to create things and it starts in our mind. Even the bible tells us that, As a man thinketh, so is he. This simply means that you are where YOU think you should be. You will never supersede a place outside of your mental reach. There is another saying that says if you can see it (meaning in your mind) then you can achieve it. This is telling us to think big and big things will happen.

The spoken word is eternal & spiritual; spoken words are spiritual seeds that go forth & are planted in the spirit realm. The word of God tells us that we shall decree (speak) a thing & it shall be established in the earth. Established means settled, fixed, rooted, and grounded. Another common scripture in the word of God that speaks to this is, "death & life are in the power of your tongue & whoever loves it shall it its fruit". This is simply saying death & life are in the power of your spoken words or cursing & blessing are in the power of your words or poverty or prosperity is in the power of your words... Do you get what that means? There's so much power in our words that clause 2 of that scripture says & they that love it shall eat its fruit... Ok so this simply means that you will have what you say but also note: Fruit by definition is the ripened reproductive body of a seeded plant. So to recap, when spoken words or spiritual seed go forth out of someone's mouth, they will be established/rooted & planted in the Earth & once they are full grown you shall have whatever **_YOU SAY,_** whether it is good or bad. That is something to definitely think about.

Now we will go into the manual...

Question: What is your gift?

Answer: _____

Question: How can the world benefit from it?

Answer: _____

Action:

To create a list of declarations that you can meditate on and speak out loud several times throughout your day.

Examples:

I was born for this….

I will walk in my greatness

The world needs (whatever you will provide)

TAKE-AWAYS:

_____

_____

_____

_____

_____

_____

_____

_____

_____

_____

SCOPE

Planning for the finished product

SCOPE DEFINED & DEFINING YOUR SCOPE

SCOPE *is what you want to create, achieve or*

produce...the 'DESIRED end.

The scope is simply what you wish to possess after crossing the finish line. This chapter will explain what the scope is and how to create one for your business, project or idea.

The scope tells you step by step, what you need to initiate the process. This is a reference document that is used to keep you on task to ensure that you do/create what you intended. The scope should break down the process step by step and will assist you in controlling what takes place and when. It can also help you manage risk and/or cost by controlling change.

First things first; we will create an itemized list of what it will take in order for you to achieve your desired outcome. This document is called a Plan of Action and Milestones (POAM). It will identify the action, the resource, the beginning date, an estimated completion date and any risk, barriers and/or concerns that may impede the process from happening smoothly.

The POAM

The POAM is a list of actions/steps that build upon each other and are necessary to your success. In the POAM each action is listed as a Task Item. Each Task Item is broken down by Resources, The Planned Beginning Date, Planned Completion Date, and Risk/Barriers/Concerns.

Resources are anything and/or anyone that is required and/or beneficial to the completion of that action. This can include any persons, databases, agencies etcetera required to complete that task. The **Planned Start Date** is the date you project that you will be able to begin working the action. You should be aware that planned dates of some of the task will be able to overlap with other task. While others can only begin after others have been completed. You will get a better look at this as you actually begin to map out your process and take an in depth look at each of the actions and it's requirements. The

Planned Completion Date is a realistic date that you plan to have the action completed. This is simply an estimate of when you'd like to have the task completed. Although you want to maintain your schedule, try to allow some flexibility so if there is a setback it will not put you in a bind. Finally, you need to list any **Risk, Barriers and/or Concerns** you foresee that may interfere in completing this action. This can be anything that causes a delay or that may prevent you from moving forward. Always review anything that arises and the immediate problem it may cause with your remaining actions. Also keep in mind to review the completed actions to ensure they will not expire or have to be reworked. Needless to say, work to find a solution ASAP. The longer it takes, the more common it is for people to become discouraged and frustrated. Do as much as you can as soon as you can. Keep moving forward.

The length and detail of the POAM will vary based on the required depth, detail and how long it will take to reach your goal.

Most often, the POAM is broken down by weeks, one month, three months, six months, nine months and one year goal dates.

A MAP

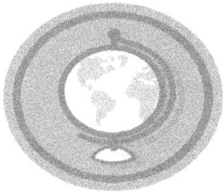

Just as the name implies, a map is often used to help us determine which way to go. Mapping out processes is used to identify the holes that may impact meeting your goals. It can be as simple or intricate as you desire but it serves the same purpose; to give you direction. Each step in the map process should be broken down to its lowest level to ensure completion. For example, if you were working on creating a price listing for products or services you will provide in your company, you may need to conduct a market analysis prior to doing this to ensure that you are offering a fair market value, you are not over/under priced and you are competitive. The step would state for you to create the price listing but in order to do this, first you would have to complete the market analysis/research. Looking at every step to this degree will help you break down the process further to ensure that you are realistic in developing your timeline to achieve your goal.

Lastly, to complete the scope portion of your project you should create a **Project Scope Statement** that will identify a detailed description of the product you want to produce or the service you intend to provide. It will be dispensed to all key persons in order to ensure that everyone is on the same page. It should contain any boundary requirements, what is an acceptable result/end item, any known constraints that may exist and the final desired outcome.

Question: Are you ready to create your plan?

Answer: _____

Question: Are you ready to serve humanity with your gifts/talents?

Answer: _____

Action: Take a minute to re-write your plan to fit the parameters identified in the POAM. Plug that information into the MAP to determine if the actions will need to be broken down into smaller

actions in order to complete the task.

TAKE-AWAYS:

_____

_____

_____

_____

_____

_____

_____

_____

(An example of a POAM)

-	PLAN of ACTION & MILESTONES (POA&M)				
Line Item	**POA&M Task Item**	**Resource**	**Planned Start Date**	**Planned Completion Date**	**Risks/Barriers Concerns**
1	Business Name, Motto/Scripture				
2	Written Vision/Concept				
3	EIN/INC.				
4	Create the Price Listing				
5	Website/Page				
6	Products (production/Purchase)				
7	Budget				
8	Marketing				
9	Personnel				
10	Contracts				
11	Contractors				
12	Resources				
13					
14					
15					

(An example of a simple map)

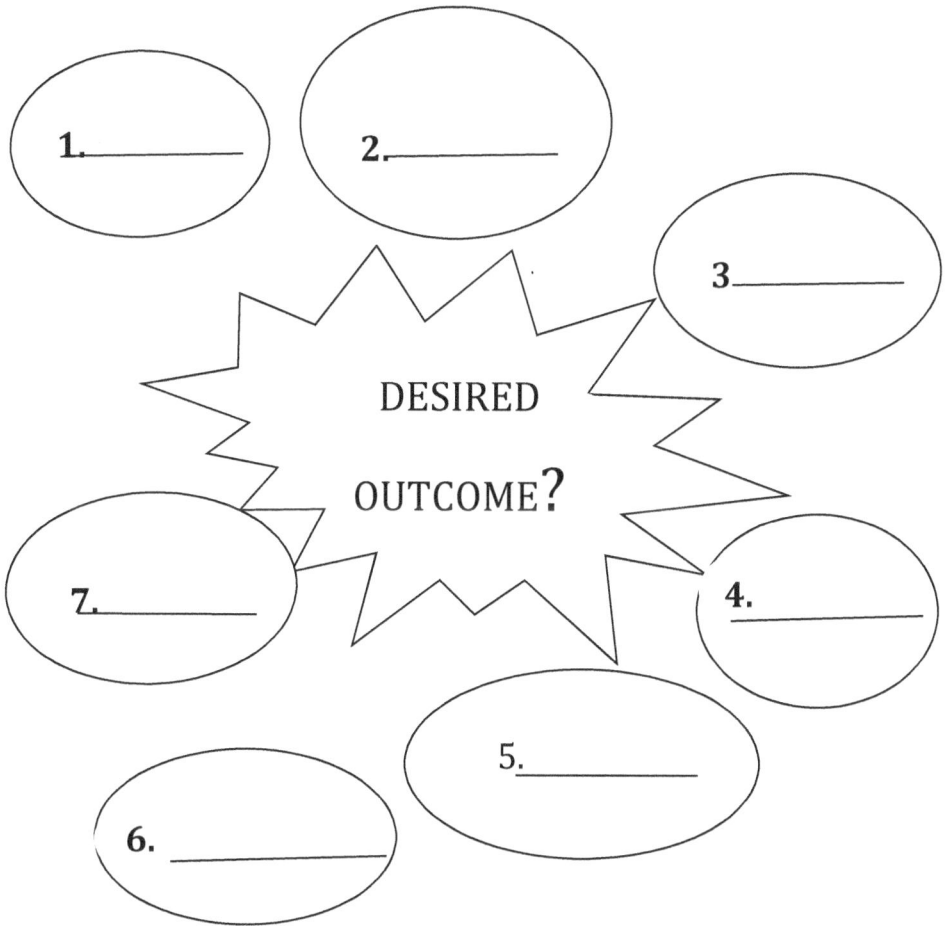

1._____

2._____

3._____

DESIRED

OUTCOME?

7._____

4._____

5._____

6. _____

RIGOROUS EXECUTION

Exact Progressive steps

Walking out YOUR Destiny…

Rigorous Execution ...*is walking out your*

Purpose with Passion

What you put into this process will determine what you get out of it. You have to set this as a priority in order to have any real lasting success and/or achievement. As the good book states, Whatsoever a man soweth THAT shall he also reap. In order to see any real results, you will have to sacrifice your time, energy and finances. In other words, **there is NO success if there is NO sacrifice.** Whatever you put your time into will yield the most results in your life. If you don't believe it then simply write down how you spend most of your time and/or energy and you will see that this area has the largest impact on your life. To be successful, you must weigh the cost because nothing less than Rigorous Execution is what is required.

Rigorous means to be done with care and attention to detail. This is where the rubber meets the road and you must carefully follow the milestones and the timeline that you have taken the time to lay out. This is where the action takes place and you determine if you were realistic in the timeframe that you set to achieve your goal. To do this, it is highly recommended that you set aside a regular time in your schedule to review your POAM several times a week as well as the progress you have and/or have not made toward completing your goal. This will help you stay aware of approaching Planned Beginning/Completion Dates so that you stay on task. It will help you remember to initiate any actions where someone else is listed as the resource so that you can plan accordingly. Always record any Barriers/Risk /Concerns that you encounter and any possible solutions. If you have a team then it's also highly recommended that you meet with them once a week as well. If distance is an issue then you can always consider using a telecomm and/or a virtual meeting space. This will help everyone stay on the same page to ensure important changes are communicated across the board. Communication is one of those things you _CAN'T_ afford to do without. It can make the difference in the outcome of your effort, the success or the failure of your goals and dreams. Try to maintain the same passion and enthusiasm from beginning to the end. Often it is when you maintain consistent momentum that you finish strong and on top.

Question: Now that you have completed the POAM and a Map, how much time are you willing to commit to executing your plans?

Answer:

_____

_____

_____

_____

TAKE-AWAYS:

_____

_____

_____

_____

_____

TAKE OWNERSHIP

Think and Act Like an Owner

Operating as the CEO…

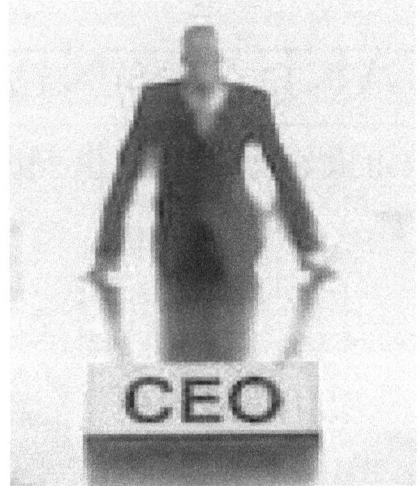

Take Ownership *recognize the RESULT of YOUR actions.*

In summation. Think like the CEO/Boss! I'd like to remind you that your mindset will determine what happens from here. Every step forward is a step closer to you realizing your goals and dreams. How you handle any setbacks will also determine how things move forward. Try and maintain a positive mindset. Setbacks simply allow us to identify the holes and gaps in our processes so that we have the opportunity to go back and rethink the process and move forward. Mediate, refocus and the solution will come.

As the CEO, you must see your goal not as it is today but as you dream/desire for it to become tomorrow. If you desire to take your business/company to the next level, begin to operate like that now. Set your team in place and begin to operate as if you are a multi-million dollar corporation. Look at the gaps and holes and areas that need improvement and implement those changes as soon as you can without risking any lost. The time is NOW! Consider the risk, weigh the cost of going the extra mile. Began to build your BRAND so that people will associate the quality you provide with YOUR name. Word of mouth is the best marketing program there is. You will find that when people can appreciate the value you provide then they will naturally want to tell someone about you and your product, your service etc. Make sure that you understand that every decision that has been made in this process and going forth will impact your progress, your growth and your success. This is YOUR time of greatness, of increase & enlargement. Walk out your purpose with passion in prosperity and I'll see YOU at the top!

Question: What happens when you destroy the box that people have for you to live in?

Answer:

_____

_____

_____

Action:

Spend focused/dedicated time tapping into your creativity (brain storming, journaling, word associations etc.) on how you can achieve your dreams and do it in a new, fun and fulfilling way.

TAKE-AWAYS:

_____

_____

_____

_____

_____

_____

_____

_____

_____

_____

_____

_____

_____

_____

_____

_____

_____

_____

About the Author

Chanda Coston is a mother, author, consultant and senior Pastor of Moving by His Spirit Ministries in Hampton, VA, and Waldorf, MD. She has a two-fold anointing; to the market place as well as the church. Her experience in corporate America has equipped her with the knowledge that she often pairs with kingdom principles for daily application. She has been gifted with the ability to teach the uneducated as well as the educated with the necessary tools to walk into their destinies. She does this by advising her clients, small business owners, ministry leaders and churches through individual consultations (one on one) and/or work-shops. You could be next! Connect with her at:

Facebook: Chanda Coston
Instagram: KingdomConcepts
Twitter: KingdomConIntl
KingdomConceptsIntl@gmx.com
(888)705-0399

www.ingramcontent.com/pod-product-compliance
Lightning Source LLC
Chambersburg PA
CBHW021914040426
42447CB00007B/858